OFF THEY GO!

This book belongs to:

_____

_____

_____

Animals in the book

BARN SWALLOW 8

HIRUNDO RUSTICA
Bird, Europe, North Africa

EMPEROR PENGUIN 10

APTENODYTES FORSTERI
Bird, Antarctica

MONARCH BUTTERFLY 12

DANAUS PLEXIPPUS
Insect, USA

LEATHERBACK SEA TURTLE 14

DERMOCHELYS CORIACEA
Reptile, Every Ocean of the World

CHRISTMAS ISLAND RED CRAB 16

GECARCOIDEA NATALIS
Crustacean, Christmas Island, Indian Ocean

SALMON 18

ONCORHYNCHUS TSHAWYTSCHA
Fish, North West America, Pacific Ocean

STRAW-COLOURED BAT 20

EIDOLON HELVUM
Mammal, Africa

HUMPBACK WHALE 22

MEGAPTERA NOVAEANGLIAE
Mammal, Every Ocean of the World

HUMAN 24

HOMO SAPIENS
Mammal, Every Continent of the World

HOW DO THEY KNOW WHERE TO GO?
Animal Navigations 28

HOW FAR FROM HERE?
Unusual Migrations 32

OFF THEY GO!

Animal Migrations

James Carter and James Munro

graffeg

Every creature
as from birth
begins its journey
here on earth

Learns to stroll
or swim or fly
to stay alive
so they'll survive

For they will need
to hunt or feed
find water, shelter
time to breed

This world over
they'll migrate
through time and space
they'll navigate

On the wing
they'll feed away
to roost by night
and fly by day

EMPEROR PENGUIN

Late March
the pair will go
a hundred miles
across the snow

With their egg
the male will wait
the winter long
to see his mate

August now
she's made her trip
she's back to feed
their brand-new chick

MONARCH BUTTERFLY

Heading north
and seeking cold
to Canada
from Mexico

First to Texas
U – S – A
where they'll have
their eggs to lay

As adults, they will further roam by winter, they'll be heading home

LEATHERBACK SEA TURTLE

For ten thousand
miles or more
they'll seek their birthplace
on a shore

Where eggs are laid
way down below
now weeks will pass
before they show

When little hatchlings
scrabble free
across the sands
into the sea

CHRISTMAS ISLAND RED CRAB

The rainy months have come around and now it's crimson on the ground

It's fifty million crabs or so scuttling, shuffling as they go

SALMON

Up the river
from the sea
swims a silver
odyssey

To one great park in Zambia from many parts of Africa

STRAW-COLOURED BAT

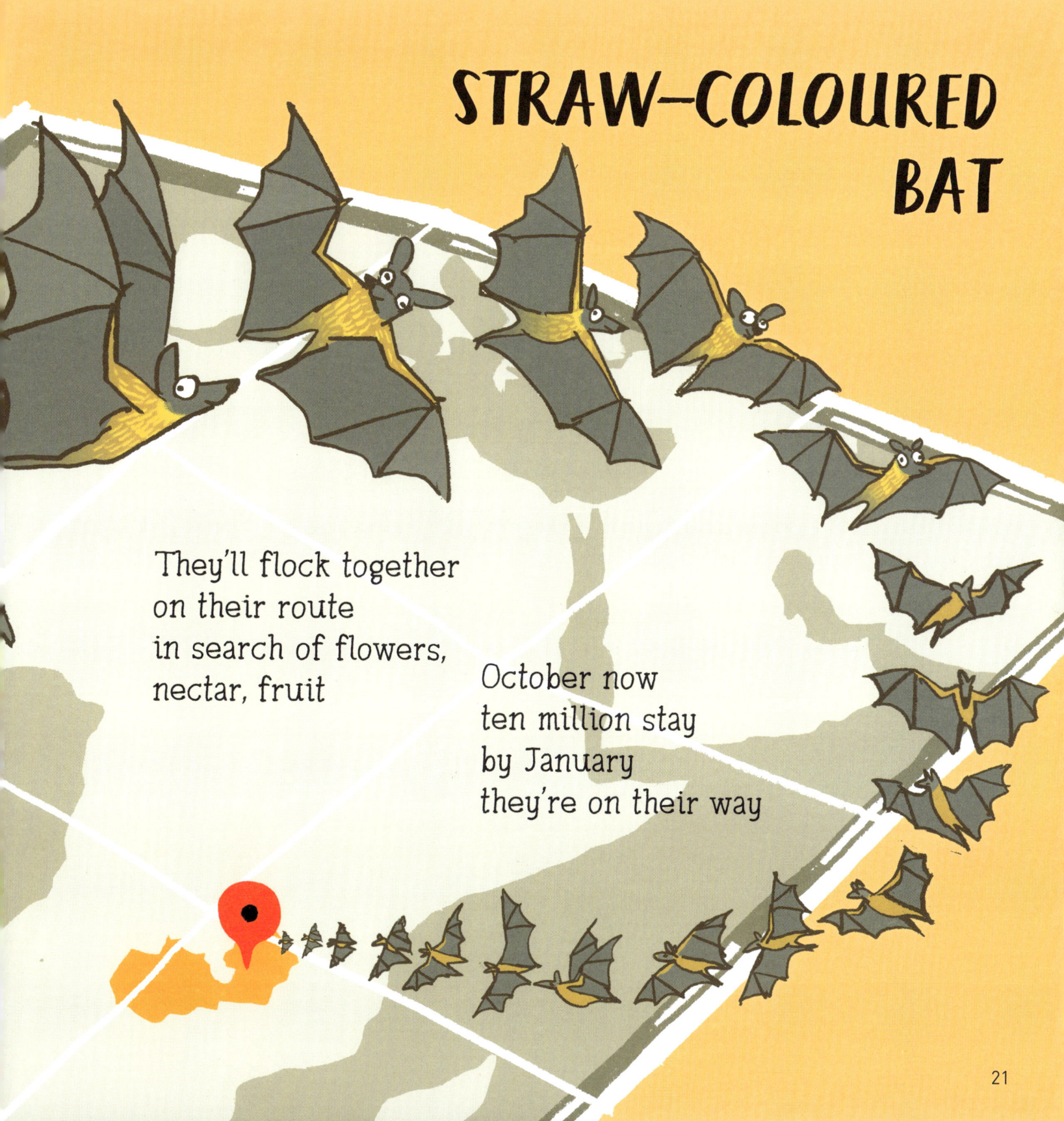

They'll flock together
on their route
in search of flowers,
nectar, fruit

October now
ten million stay
by January
they're on their way

When journeys just go on and on what better than to swim in song?

HUMPBACK WHALE

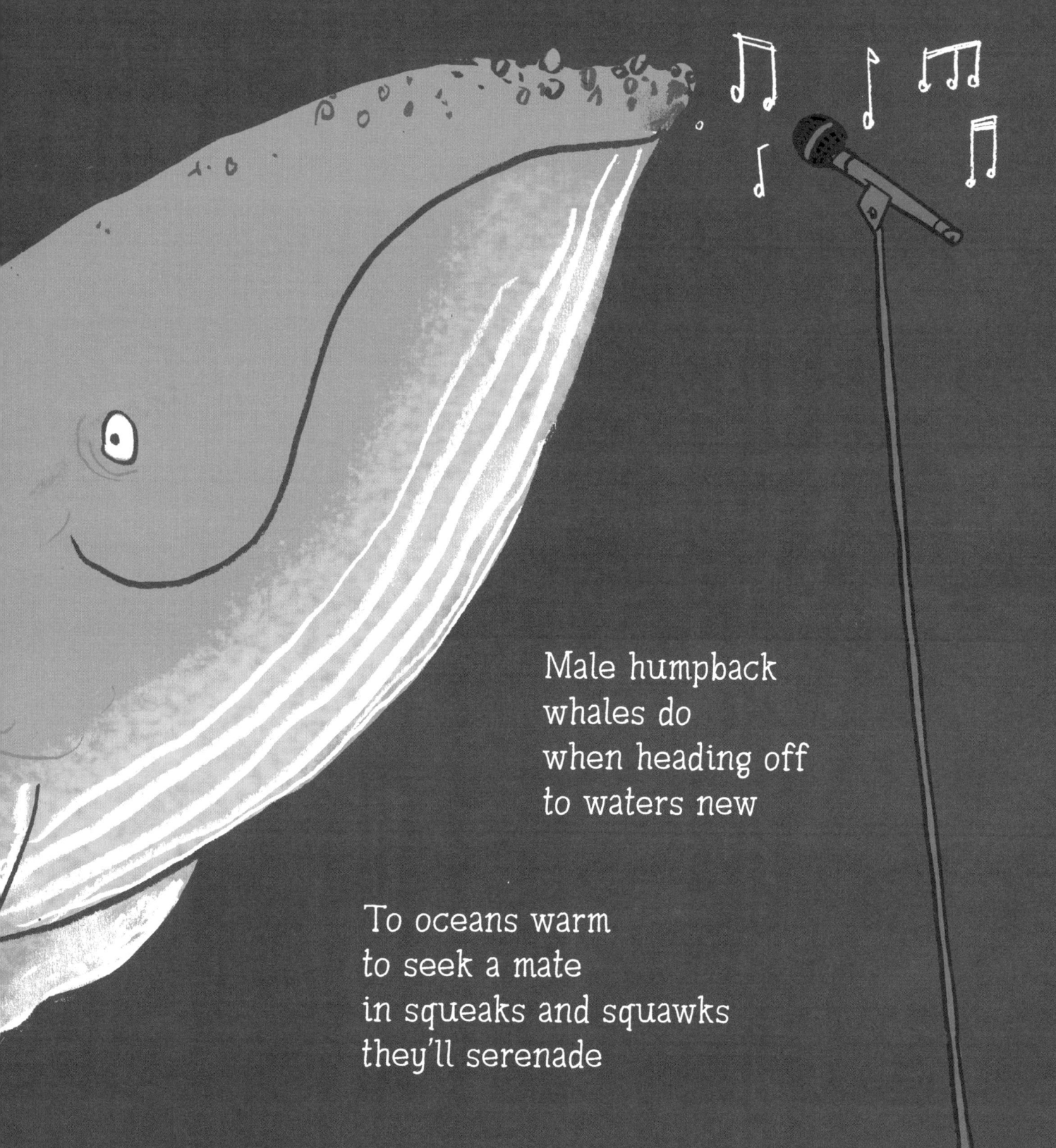

Male humpback
whales do
when heading off
to waters new

To oceans warm
to seek a mate
in squeaks and squawks
they'll serenade

HUMAN

Before the boat
the plane the car
us humans learnt
to venture far

From Africa
where we began
we walked the world
from land to land

But now we travel
every day
hey, human –
where've you been today?

All continents
all skies and oceans
ever spinning
world in motion

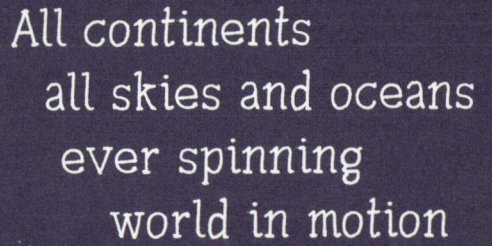

Everything
and everyone
revolves each year
around the sun

Thus seasons turn
bring change and so
those journeys start
and

OFF THEY GO !

HOW DO THEY KNOW WHERE TO GO?
ANIMAL NAVIGATIONS

Dung beetles are thought to be guided home by the glow of the Milky Way in the night sky above. And one type of dung beetle is known to travel home at night with the aid of moonlight.

How amazing is it that creatures can find their way from one place on this planet to another by just looking up at the sky? More incredible is that these animals have all in turn worked out how to do it by themselves!

Birds like indigo buntings migrate after dark so that they can be guided by the rotation of the stars – and in particular around Polaris, the North Star. Indeed, animals of all kinds navigate by the stars and the Moon – from seals to turtles to frogs.

Some birds journey by day and use the sun as a compass by which to lead them to their various destinations. The benefit of journeying in daylight is that these migrating birds can ride on the thermals – currents of warm air created by the sun heating the ground, and in turn heating the air above.

THE LANDSCAPE can also help migration – for example, with visual clues such as mountains, valleys, rivers and coastlines, even buildings – and creatures can internalise these features in their memories, which become INTERNAL MENTAL MAPS.

Scientists believe that there are birds that have an internal compass device which allows them to navigate by what is known as the EARTH'S MAGNETIC FIELD. So even on a first flight they will be able to find their way to their destination. Clever or what?

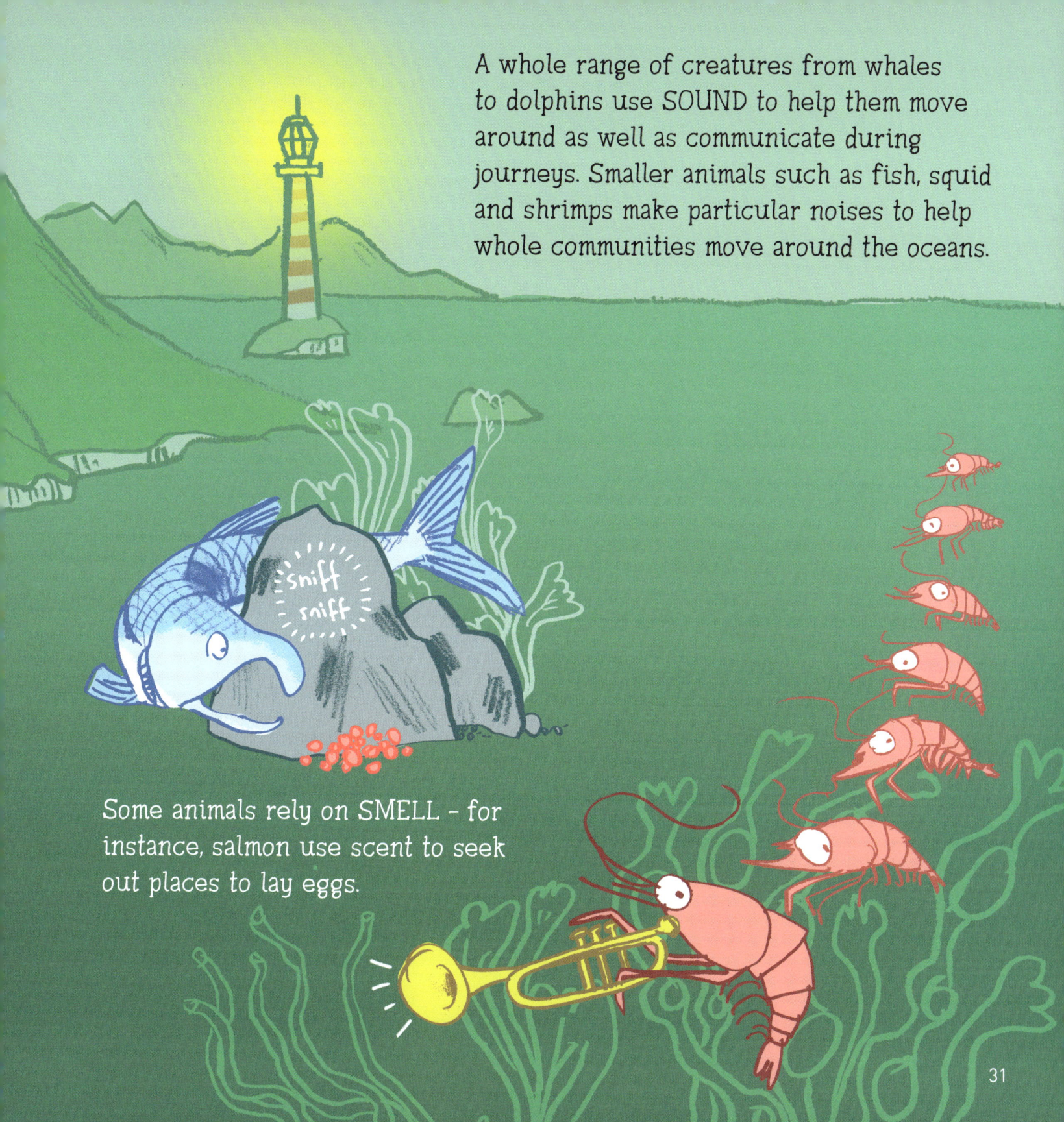

A whole range of creatures from whales to dolphins use SOUND to help them move around as well as communicate during journeys. Smaller animals such as fish, squid and shrimps make particular noises to help whole communities move around the oceans.

Some animals rely on SMELL - for instance, salmon use scent to seek out places to lay eggs.

HOW FAR FROM HERE?
UNUSUAL MIGRATIONS

SEEN NUFFIN' OF A PUFFIN?
In summer, puffins can be spotted diving into the sea, gathering sand eels for their young. But in winter they disappear, heading off up to the North Sea or down to the Atlantic coast off France. At times they are known to form giant rafts on the ocean – thousands of them at a time – to protect themselves against predators.

DAY TRIPPERS! Microscopic sea creatures known as zoo plankton sink to deep water at dawn, then rise back up to near the surface at sunset. Scientists call this 'diel vertical migration'. It's the biggest of all daily migrations and it's done by billions of billions of these tiny critters! It's believed they go to the surface to feed and head down below to avoid being eaten by predators. Golden jellyfish make small migrations of their own, following the course of the sun throughout a day.

CAN YOU B-EEL-IEVE IT?
For years, no one knew where the eels from the European rivers disappeared to every autumn. Now we have discovered they head all the way down to the Sargasso Sea in the Atlantic Ocean. What is unusual is that they change colour as they journey back to Europe – from clear to yellow to silver – as they mature from new-born elvers to fully adult eels.

KEEP OFF THE ROAD!
Like their cousins the toads, frogs will migrate to nearby places to feed, reproduce or hibernate. Other amphibians make small journeys: on spring nights the salamanders of Canada are known to move from their underground habitats to small ponds to breed, though many can get squashed by vehicles on roads along the way.

HOW FAR CAN A DRAGONFLY FLY? Far! Well, one dragonfly – the globe skimmer – can journey up to 6,000 kilometres. They will travel on the winds from India, across the Indian Ocean, stopping off to lay eggs on various islands along the way. Those newly hatched dragonflies will continue the migration to Africa. By the rainy season, they start heading back to India.

THIRSTY WORK! How far would you go to get a drink? In Africa, herds of up to one and a half million wildebeest travel as far as 800 kilometres for water each year. They are joined along the way by other mammals like antelopes and zebras. Both African and Asian elephants are also on the move in those drier seasons, seeking out lakes, rivers and waterholes.

For Heather Cuny and Rhona Ritchie and all the pupils of two fabulous schools – École Sartoux and École Trois Collines in the south of France.
J.C.

For my family living in far-flung corners of the globe whose skies still share the same swallows.
J.M.

Off They Go!

Published in Great Britain in 2025 by Graffeg Limited.

ISBN 9781802588156

Text by James Carter copyright © 2025.
Illustrations by James Munro copyright © 2025.
Designed and produced by Graffeg Limited copyright © 2025.

Graffeg Limited, 15 Neptune Court, Vanguard Way, Cardiff, CF24 5PJ, Wales, UK. Tel: 01554 824000. croeso@graffeg.com. www.graffeg.com

James Carter and James Munro are hereby identified as the author and the illustrator of this work in accordance with section 77 of the Copyright, Designs and Patents Act 1988.

Printed by FINIDR, s.r.o., Czechia.

A CIP Catalogue record for this book is available from the British Library.

All rights reserved. No part of this publication may be reproduced, stored in a retrieval system or transmitted, in any form or by any means, electronic, mechanical, photocopying, recording or otherwise, without the prior permission of the publishers.

This book is designed for children, printed with materials and processes that are safe and meet all applicable European safety requirements. The book does not contain elements that could pose health or safety risks under normal and intended use.

We hereby declare that this product complies with all applicable requirements of the General Product Safety Regulation (GPSR) and any other relevant EU legislation.

Appointed EU Representative:
Easy Access System Europe Oü, 16879218
Mustamäe tee 50, 10621, Tallinn, Estonia
gpsr.requests@easproject.com

The publisher gratefully acknowledges the financial support of this book by the Books Council of Wales. www.gwales.com

1 2 3 4 5 6 7 8 9